last straw strategies

giving up those bottles, blankies, pacifiers, and so on . . .

letting go

Michelle Kennedy

D0170470

BARRON'S

First edition for the United States, its territories
and possessions, and Canada published in 2004 by
BARRON'S EDUCATIONAL SERIES, INC.
by arrangement with
THE IVY PRESS LIMITED

All inquiries should be addressed to:
Barron's Educational Series, Inc.,
250 Wireless Boulevard
Hauppauge, New York 11788
www.barronseduc.com

© THE IVY PRESS LIMITED, 2004

All rights reserved. Without limiting the rights
under copyright reserved above, no part of this
publication may be reproduced, stored in or
introduced into a retrieval system, or transmitted, in
any form or by any means (electronic, mechanical,
photocopying, recording, or otherwise), without the
prior written permission of both the copyright
holder and the publisher of this book.

Every effort has been taken to ensure that all
information in this book is correct. This book is not
intended to replace consultation with your doctor,
surgeon, or other healthcare professional. The author
and publisher disclaim any loss, injury, or damage
incurred as a consequence, directly or indirectly, of
the use and application of the contents of this book.

International Standard Book Number
0-7641-2721-7

Library of Congress Catalog Card No.
2003107788

This book was conceived,
designed, and produced by
THE IVY PRESS LIMITED
The Old Candlemakers
West Street
Lewes
East Sussex BN7 2NZ

Creative Director PETER BRIDGEWATER
Publisher SOPHIE COLLINS
Editorial Director STEVE LUCK
Design Manager TONY SEDDON
Project Editor MANDY GREENFIELD
Designer JANE LANAWAY
Illustrator EMMA BROWNJOHN

Printed in China by
Hong Kong Graphics & Printing Ltd.
9 8 7 6 5 4 3 2 1

contents

letting go
introduction

Sometimes, in the great cycle of feeding, cuddling, and clothing, you lose sight of the objective of brood-rearing: to watch them leave the nest. Although this will not happen literally for another couple of decades (if ever, in some cases), yet another of your parental duties is to teach your kids how to let go of things they don't need any more and how to deal with independence. It is best to start early, with small doses of autonomy, so that you raise confident kids who know that they can meet any challenge and assume the responsibilities expected of them.

It's difficult to make hard-and-fast rules, since each child is different, at different ages. For every determined toddler in the mall, screaming to escape her stroller, there is the four-year-old who needs her security blanket in her backpack—

sometimes they are even the same child. As long as the degree of freedom is appropriate to age, circumstance, and safety, it should be okay. Here are hints—from moms, dads, and grandparents just like us—that should ensure independence is reached painlessly, both for you and your child.

blankets and
favorite toys

You alternately love them and hate them. Those blankets, stuffed animals, or other "loveys," as well-known author and pediatrician Dr. T. Berry Brazelton calls them, are either the bane of your parenting existence or your savior during that car trip gone awry. You may never understand just why your children adore these objects so much, but you can try. You also need to examine, when trying to separate your children from such objects, if you are truly doing it for them—or for yourself because of the discomfort they can cause you. It's hard to admit, but sometimes those smelly "blankies" are just a little embarrassing at a fancy restaurant. No problem—these tips should help you cope with your child's dependence on them and, hopefully, get him to slowly let them go.

the blankie fairy

Your child has had that old blanket since the day she came home from hospital. It's tattered and torn and has not been washed in months. You are desperate to replace it with a new one, but your child will know the difference. Maryland-based author Carol Seefeldt suggests the Blankie Fairy. Because children believe in Santa Claus and the Tooth Fairy, a Blankie Fairy is not so far-fetched. It could magically come in one night and leave a new blanket in place of the old one.

the power of smell

Part, and sometimes all, of the attraction of a particular blanket or stuffed animal is the smell. If your child's "cuddly" is becoming a bit of an embarrassment, a good plan might be to sneak a replica into bed with her each night for a week or so. (Buy a replacement as soon as you realize it's "the one," for if you wait too long, it may be impossible to find an exact replica.) This way the new one will take on that familiar cuddly smell and will be easier to pass off as the same toy.

a lost blankie

A child who has lost her blankie can be absolutely inconsolable. One mother said that after a week of searching in stores with her child for a similar blanket—without luck—she then explained to her daughter that as people grow older, they get different types of blankets. The girl finally picked out a new blanket, but the mom reported that it never left her bed and she never formed the same type of attachment to anything else. While this mom laments her daughter's loss a little, many parents might exalt in their child's new-found independence.

the old switcheroo

One mom described a great way to introduce a replacement blanket to her son. She bought an identical blanket when she noticed the old one getting worn out and, when it came time to make the switch, inspiration struck. She put both in the wash together, and when they came out of the dryer she ran to her son exclaiming, "The dryer fixed your blankie!" He tested the blanket, smelled it, and found it just as worthy.

what is its appeal?

Find out, if you can, what is so appealing about this particular item. You might think, author Vicki Iovine says, that the reason your child is so attached to a particular stuffed animal is because it is cute and has its own TV show. Think again! Your child might just be in love with the satiny label on the back and how it feels when he rubs it between his fingers. (My own children have never been particularly attached to anything, sleeping only occasionally with a new toy like a perfectly uncuddly plastic Rescue Hero.) Some children cannot articulate the appeal of a loved object, but for those who can, finding out what is so appealing about it can go a long way toward helping to find a replacement, or perhaps even ending the dependence.

passing it down

You will be surprised by what your child can understand. Simply explain to her that blankies are for younger kids and that it would be great if she could give it to a younger brother or sister—or perhaps a family friend who is having a baby. Most children will be happy to wrap it up and give it away as a present, but be careful. Some children might get a little "stage fright" the moment they are supposed to give it away. A small present as a reward for generosity can help a child who is having trouble giving away her blankie, especially if the act of giving is just a little too much for her at that moment.

washing the need away 2-5 years

Washing a favorite blankie or stuffed animal can be a great way to wean your child of his need for it. I know of more than a few children who gradually began to leave their

comfort objects behind after a cycle through the washer and dryer. Sure, they still felt good, but without that smell, they just didn't satisfy in the same way. Look out, though, because your favorite sweater could become the next "cuddly."

favorite toys

accept the magic

Trying to force your child to give up a "cuddly" can only make things worse. Think of your child's comfort object as a way to bring a bit of you and home along with him in that big, scary world, making him feel more secure and protected. Often children with such objects are more adventurous and outgoing because they know that in their backpack or in their cubby is a little piece of home. Accepting their need for the object, and not making a big deal about it, will not only make your child less self-conscious about needing the toy, but will let them know that you appreciate their need for a "mommy stand-in" when you're away. Children who are allowed to bring their cuddlies along are also less likely to need them as they get older because less emphasis has been placed on them.

little pieces

One way to let your child take a bit of her "cuddly" everywhere is to cut a small piece from it (with her permission of course). This little piece can then be kept in her pocket while she's at school or at a friend's house, and when she is feeling a little lonely, she can feel it in her pocket or take it out to look at.

2-5 years

a picture's worth a thousand words

One mom said she took a picture of her child's blanket lying on his bed waiting for him, and let him take the photo to school. This offers an alternative to cutting a piece from the blanket. A great way to present the idea to your child is to say that you are worried about the blanket getting lost and that this way he can look at it all day, secure in the knowledge that it is safe at home on his bed.

set realistic
favorite toys
limits   2-5 years

You must be careful when deciding to take away a comfort object—and I really don't recommend doing so, since I am more of the, "If it's not broken . . . " kind of mom. However, if you must, start by restricting where and when your child can have his "cuddly." Perhaps say yes to the car, but no to taking it to the store. Say yes to the bedroom, but no to the backyard. This will at least initiate the process of learning to leave it behind, again with constant reassurance from you that the item is just fine in its designated place, and will still be there when your little one returns.

bottles

Children older than two who are still using a bottle are probably using it more as a comfort object than as a nutrition source. Because the bottle is now a friend and possibly a forceful habit, it will be difficult to get her to give it up. You have to make a choice as to whether you do not mind substituting something like a blanket or doll for the bottle, or whether you want her to go "cold turkey." Either way, it will take some time. But remember that most experts say that too much bottle use—particularly as children get into their third and fourth years—can deform their mouths and teeth.

start early

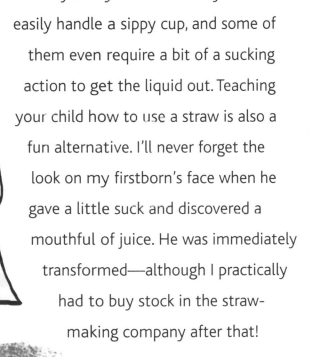

bottles

1-2 years

If you can, try to get your child to give up the bottle at a fairly young age—as early as a year old. A one-year-old can easily handle a sippy cup, and some of them even require a bit of a sucking action to get the liquid out. Teaching your child how to use a straw is also a fun alternative. I'll never forget the look on my firstborn's face when he gave a little suck and discovered a mouthful of juice. He was immediately transformed—although I practically had to buy stock in the straw-making company after that!

enlist his help

bottles

One great way to include your little one in giving up the

bottle is to cut a deal with him. Set a date sometime in the

near future and start a countdown to bottle-free day. Make

a pact out of it—let your child start a collection of each

bottle that he finishes and, when the day arrives, let him take his collection of emptied bottles to a special store and "purchase" whatever he wants with the bottles (sometimes shopkeepers are a great help in this). He can then carry his new skates, or whatever, home, knowing that he made a

good swap. If he asks you about the bottles, just remind him gently about what happened. If he wants a "refund," tell him the store sold those bottles to a much younger baby because he didn't need them anymore.

bottles

her own cup

Sometimes your little one isn't so much averse to the idea of drinking from a cup, but simply doesn't want to share . . . and why should she? She's been drinking out of bottles that belonged to her for a very long time, and it's possible she is feeling a little possessive and doesn't want to let them go. This is a good time to take her on a special shopping trip. Most children's sections of department stores sell goods devoted to the transition phase, where you will find all kinds of "sippy" cups. I found that the best ones had no handles and snap-on lids. Let your child pick out one cup that is solely for her use—it might have a special cartoon character on it or be a special color. Letting her choose it and then pay for it at the register is a great way to get her involved. And buy something to fill it up with right away, so that she doesn't lose interest in it on the way home!

less and less

bottles

2-4 years

If you decide to take a more gradual approach to letting go of the bottle, begin to fill it with less liquid—and only water—every night. By the end of a week there should be very little water in the bottle. Nighttime bottles should only contain water anyway, once your baby is old enough not to need formula or breast milk as his main source of nutrition, to prevent tooth decay. Sometimes just filling a bottle with water will encourage a child to drop it—quite literally!

water in the bottle, juice in my cup

It's kind of a bribe, I know, but sometimes you just can't beat 'em! Whenever your child asks for her bottle, give her only water in it, even if she's asked for juice or milk. Tell her that if she wants something else, she has to drink it from

a cup. Don't make a huge deal out of it. Just inform her matter-of-factly, "That's how we drink our juice, in a cup." Most kids will drink water, and I wholeheartedly encourage it, but when trying to let go of the bottle, sometimes the allure of something sweet is just too powerful—so make sure you use it to your advantage!

2-4 years **replace the bottle**

Have your child choose a favorite stuffed animal or blanket that she will take in place of her bottle. Sometimes, children will accept even the bluntest terms. Tell her simply that it's time to give up the bottle because she is older now, but emphasize that if she needs something to sleep with at night, she can select one of her cuddly toys or, if you want to give her an incentive, a new one from the toy store. Make sure to include the new "cuddly" in your current nighttime rituals in the same way you did with the bottle.

the high chair

bottles

2-4 years

This is not meant as a punishment, but more as an association. If your child demands a bottle, then make him sit in the high chair while he drinks it. Don't offer any explanation like, "Babies who drink from bottles sit in high chairs," because he will reach that conclusion on his own. On the flip side, if he accepts a cup, let him have free rein in the kitchen.

bottles
2-4 years   **cold turkey**

Just make an announcement one day. Be direct and matter-of-fact about it and state that he is now a big boy (this is especially helpful if he is already potty-trained or going through the process) and big boys drink from cups—just like mommy and daddy. You might even be

able to get him to help you pack up the bottles for storage. This is much better than having him wake up to a bottle-free household one morning. If he is "in the know" and can participate, he is much less likely to ask for the bottles back —or, at least, he will understand where they went when you say no. But be prepared for a bit of crankiness or even a full-blown temper tantrum. The key is not to give in, but to find suitable replacements, like sippy cups or straws, for the bottle.

bottles

can't do cold turkey?

Then try to gradually replace the bottles one at a time. Replace the least important ones first, with a sippy cup or straw travel bottle. The lunchtime bottle is usually the first to go, then the nap-time or quiet-time bottles. Give it some time before you replace the morning or bedtime bottles. You might find that eventually your child just doesn't "need" those quite as much anymore as she becomes accustomed to the feel of a cup.

peer pressure   2-4 years

If your child goes to a day care center where some of the
other children use bottles, then it will be easier to wait
until vacation time or even a weekend to start replacing
the bottle. Peer pressure is a powerful thing, and if everyone
else has a bottle, it will be hard for your little one to give up

hers. However, if the other
children don't use bottles,
it could inspire your
child, even without
prompting from you.

bottles

let her keep the bottles

2-4 years

"What?" you say, "keep them?" Yes. Let your child keep one or two of her bottles, but without anything in them and only to carry around, to suck on with nothing in them, or

to "feed" to a favorite doll or stuffed animal. Just having them around, like a favorite blanket, can be of great comfort to a child. You can even let her sleep with them as long as she knows they will never again be filled with milk or any other drink. And, just like a blanket or stuffed animal, eventually she will lose interest.

pacifiers

The pacifier is really a wonderful thing. Most experts agree that pacifiers are a great way to satisfy an infant's need to suck. They can be comforting at bedtime and can quiet a baby during a car ride or trip to the store. But what happens when the infant pacifier-user turns into a toddler and perhaps even a preschooler? When is enough, enough? That's really for you to decide—and if you have determined that sucking has become a habit rather than a need, then the following tips should assist you in helping your child drop it.

offer a knuckle
instead 3 months–1 year

If you are worried your infant will become addicted to the
pacifier, then don't introduce her to one. I easily transferred
my second baby from my breast to my (clean) knuckle when

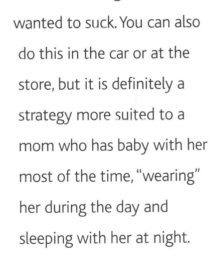

it was obvious she was done feeding, but still

wanted to suck. You can also
do this in the car or at the
store, but it is definitely a
strategy more suited to a
mom who has baby with her
most of the time, "wearing"
her during the day and
sleeping with her at night.

pacifiers

get a routine

Some moms complain that their baby actually prefers the binky to the breast. Renowned pediatrician Dr. William Sears offers these tips in response:

- Feed him more frequently. Sucking on a pacifier won't meet your baby's nutritional needs.

- Eliminate distractions during nursing. At this age, your infant's more acute vision makes him more

easily distracted during nursing, so that he becomes Mr. Suck-a-Little-Look-a-Little. At feeding time, take him into a quiet room and get down to the business of nursing.

🖐 Establish a routine. A daily nap-nursing routine has worked for our family. At least twice a day, lie down with your baby and nap-nurse—much like you did when he was a newborn. This peaceful reconnection in a quiet room is likely to bring him back to the breast.

🖐 Offer your finger. Periodically, let your baby suck on your finger instead of the pacifier—even during the nap-nursing time—if he doesn't want to feed.

pacifiers

pull the plug before it becomes a habit

1–4 years

According to Dr. Sears: "Ideally, pacifiers are for the comfort of babies, not the convenience of parents (but I have yet to meet the ideal parent or the ideal baby) . . . To insert the plug and leave the baby in the plastic infant seat every time he cries is unhealthy reliance on an artificial comforter. This baby needs picking up and holding. A person should always be at the other end of a comforting tool. The breast (or the

finger) has the built-in advantage of making sure you don't fall into the habit of just plugging up the source of the cries as a mechanical gesture." If you find yourself automatically reaching for the pacifier instead of your baby when your little one cries, pull the plug before it becomes a habit.

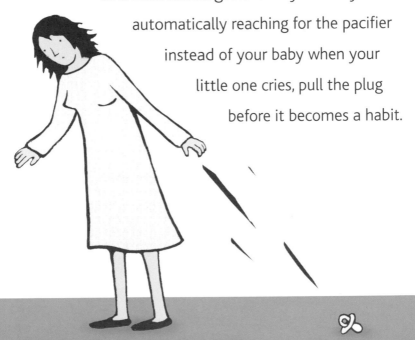

pacifiers

let it
wear out

One mom says, "Laura had her 'binky' until she was about four and 'somehow' it started to disintegrate until there was nothing left to suck on. I had talked to my pediatrician much earlier and he felt it would be too traumatic to try to take it from her at the time. She never really asked for another, but continued to sleep holding the worn-out one. One thing I know about my daughter is that change doesn't come easy for her." However, be aware that a damaged pacifier can represent a choking hazard, and ensure that no small pieces can come loose from it before allowing your child to retain it.

make it hard to find

2–4 years

When she starts to look for her pacifier, engage her in such a fun activity that she forgets her rubber friend. Then, arrange for the pacifier to be permanently "lost," substituting other touches of comfort, such as lots of snuggling and a few cuddly toys.

pacifiers

2-4 years

trash it together

My first son was in love with his pacifiers. He was given one in the nursery in the hospital and I couldn't get him to give it back! At first, he would take almost any kind of pacifier, but as he got older he became brand-specific, and then at two years old, he had one left and would accept no substitute. Eventually, the thing wore out and got just plain icky. When the rubber began to come apart, I knew we had to lose it (I didn't want him to swallow pieces of it or choke on it). I tried desperately to get him attached to another one, but no go. Finally, I sat down with him and showed him the decrepit old thing. I explained that it was dangerous and we would have to throw it away. I asked him if he wanted to do it. He said yes and we ceremoniously made our way to the trash compactor. He plopped it in and turned the knob to smush it with the other trash (a fun experience in itself). After waving good-bye one last time, he never asked for another pacifier.

pacifiers
2-4 years   **give rewards**

Praise and reward your child when she does not use a
pacifier. Star charts, daily rewards, and gentle reminders,
especially during the daytime
hours, can be very helpful without
putting too much
pressure on your
little one.

limit times

This is a good tip for overcoming most habits, and a great way to limit or reduce pacifier use. Tell your child that she can only have the pacifier at certain times of the day. Determine which times of day she needs it most—bedtime, naptime, in the car, when she gets to daycare—and then restrict her to those times. Get a little plastic cup with an easy-to-use, snap-on lid, and tell her that when she is done with the pacifier at these times, she needs to put it in the cup. Restricting the times when your child can use the pacifier will help her to realize that she doesn't need it anymore—without turning you into the bad guy!

pacifiers

go with it

Sometimes it is easiest to accept the pacifier, bottle, or whatever works best, and it will eventually be substituted for something else. One mom says, "I was an avid thumbsucker until I was eight. I had two parents and a relatively stable home. I assure you that it's no big deal. I never had braces or major personality disorders. Self-soothing is a fine art that should be encouraged. Too many people never learn this and

turn to outside sources (food, alcohol, drugs) as adults. My own son self-weaned at nine months when he discovered the pleasures of finger food. Once he was dry, he began teething with a vengeance and wanted to suck, suck, suck . . .

He very quickly gave the pacifier up, but still, at two, loves his bottle, now filled with soy milk or 1%."

pacifiers

nighttime habit

As you start to wean your child from the pacifier, continue letting him drift off to sleep with it. But once he's deep in dreamland, ease it out of his mouth. If he has a strong sleep-pacifier association, however, he may need something to help him back to sleep when he wakes in the middle of the night. Introduce some alternative non-oral "pacifiers," like a cuddly teddy bear or favorite blanket. In time, the stuffed animal should replace the pacifier as your child's bedtime companion of choice.

a couple of "nevers"

pacifiers

I have read and heard from many mothers who advocate clipping the tip off of a pacifier to make it "unsuckable." Please, please, a thousand times please, don't do this. It is an extreme choking hazard. Some pacifiers depend on that vacuum to keep them stable in their plastic holder (or whatever you call it). When you clip the tip, you release that air, and as the child sucks harder to get it to work, she can suck it right down her throat. Little pieces can also start to come off the sides. Also, never tie a pacifier around a child's neck (or wrist) or to the side of a crib or bed to prevent losing it . . . a child could easily strangle.

thumb sucking

There are as many different schools of thought on thumb sucking as there are on potty training. Thumb sucking is often praised, because the thumb is already attached to the baby and he can self-comfort. At the same time, pediatricians and dentists say that it is bad for the formation of young teeth. Some parents approve and some just hate it. Whatever your thoughts on thumb sucking, some children will just overrule you and do it anyway. But if you are really concerned that your child will suck his thumb in kindergarten (and he wouldn't be the only one) or are already having issues with his teeth (although my seven-year-old son never sucked his thumb and still has the most crooked teeth I have ever seen!), then these tips should help you get the thumb out of his mouth.

ignore it

Thumb sucking should be considered normal before the age of four years and usually ignored, especially when your child is tired or sick. In fact, during the first six months of life it can be actively encouraged as a means of self-comfort. However, if your child only sucks her thumb when she is bored, and she is older than one year, try to distract her. Give her something to do with her hands without mentioning your concern about the thumb sucking. Occasionally praise your child for not sucking her thumb.

thumb sucking
this won't work for boys, but . . .

Some girls love nail polish even more than they love thumb sucking. When one mom told her preschooler that sucking

her fingers would wear her nail polish off, she made her choose—polish or thumb sucking. Heading to school and seeing other girls with pretty pink nails helped her to choose the nail polish.

thumb sucking

keep those
hands occupied

2-5 years

From Ann Douglas, author and mom: "Try to come up with creative ways of keeping his hands busy at those times of day when his thumb tends to find its way into his mouth. If, for example, your toddler is in the habit of sucking his thumb while you read him a bedtime story, give him two small toys to hold onto—one for each hand. This approach tends to be more effective than putting a bandage or a bitter substance on your child's thumb or constantly nagging him about his behavior, strategies that can actually backfire by reinforcing the thumb sucking behavior."

thumb sucking

bribery

2-5 years ## to the rescue

Once again, some parents have had success using the reward method to discourage thumb sucking. For every day that the thumb wasn't sucked, one mom gave her son an immediate reward—like cash toward a special present or a treat. The sucking had to stop for at least 10 days to believe the habit was "reliably" broken. Once a reward was earned, it was his to keep whether the sucking ended completely or not; after several attempts the method worked and the thumb stayed out for good. This mother also suggests checking on the child for nighttime sucking and gently removing fingers if they are in the mouth.

when bribes
don't work

2-5 years

Some children just don't respond to bribes. They will try hard for a while, maybe until that special item is earned, but then they are right back to their old habits. Try putting socks over your child's hands at night. This has worked for many children. Another deterrent is a big, gaudy plastic ring on a child's sucking thumb, which can act as a reminder not to suck.

the thumbguard

There is a commercially made guard that can be strapped on a child's wrist and put over her thumb (there is also one for fingers). The device, I have been told, absolutely prevents a

child from sucking her thumb. It has been recommended by some dentists who are particularly worried about thumb sucking over the age of four or five. I have no personal experience of the device, but since it's impossible to get off, it could be a good solution for very avid thumbsuckers who pull socks or gloves off their hands. It is an FDA-approved device and can be found at: *www.thumbguard.com*

the straight elbow

Another technique is to wrap an Ace or stretch bandage
(not too tight) around the arm from a few inches below
to a few inches above the elbow. Apply it while the elbow is
straight. Then whenever your child starts to bring his thumb
toward his mouth, the pressure at his elbow will increase
and remind him to return his arm to the straight position.
It should be your child's responsibility to put on the
bandage or to ask you for assistance in doing so. Help
your child to look upon this method as a clever idea
rather than as a penalty or punishment.

thumb sucking
call in the professionals

Parents can nag day in and day out and fail to persuade a
toddler to break the habit, but a doctor or a pediatric dentist
may only need to say, "It's time to stop
sucking your thumb because it's going
to make your teeth and mouth
crooked," to inspire
her to quit.

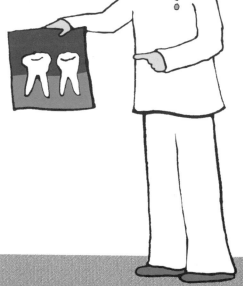

find the
motivator

2-5 years

Children can't be forced to give up a habit. They have to actually want to do it. Motivation can be inspired by the words of a professional, a parent, or another adult, by the teasing of friends or peers, by a sense of embarrassment about the habit, or even by a desire to be more grown up, but there must be motivation from within. Talk to your child about quitting. Discuss with him when would be a good time to quit, and whether a cold-turkey or a go-slow approach is more appealing to him.

thumb sucking
"big boy" praise

Don't call your toddler's sucking habits "babyish," but
do take every opportunity to call attention to "big boy"
(or "big girl") behavior, such as using the toilet, buttoning
a shirt, picking up clothes from the floor, or climbing
the jungle gym without help from an adult. The more
appreciation and praise the child garners for being grown
up, the more incentive there will be for him to act in a
grown-up fashion, and to kick bad habits such as thumb
sucking that are left over from babyhood.

keep talking

Keeping your toddler's mouth occupied with conversation, song, a musical instrument, or drinks from a straw may satisfy some of the need for oral gratification and will help to distract him from cravings for the thumb. At the times of day when your toddler tends to like to suck most, provide nourishing snacks that require a lot of chewing, but be careful that you don't overfeed or replace one oral habit with another.

"do it myself"

It can be so maddening. Your once reasonably pleasant baby has turned into a self-righteous toddler. And while you want to encourage her independence, it is also hard not to recognize that there are some things she just can't do. The best part? She's starting to get some attitude about it, too. All of a sudden your gentle guidance is met with a, "I can do it myself," or maybe even a full-blown tantrum! How do you encourage her independence and still affirm your role as, well, parent in charge? This is a good time to instill self-confidence in your child. Taking the time now to show her that you are confident in her abilities (or almost abilities) will lay the groundwork for a happy start to school life and making friends. These tips should help her on her way and help you keep your sanity.

"do it myself"

don't rescue your child 1-4 years

(Or at least not all of the time.) It is tempting to rush over and help as soon as your child runs into a little resistance. Whether it's trying to put on her shirt or doing a puzzle, let her work out some problems on her own before you step in. However, you also have to make sure she knows you're there

for her if the going gets really tough—say, when her head is stuck in the armhole of her shirt! It's a tough line we teeter on: letting her have a go, but know you will be there in a pinch.

"do it myself"

avoid

power struggles

Asking him an open-ended question about what he wants
to drink is only setting yourself up for a power struggle.
So ask simply, "Do you want milk or apple juice with lunch?"
If you can, keep your drinks in containers that he can safely
pour, like a pitcher with a secure lid and
a small pouring spout. This will not
only allow him to make the choice,
but also pour it by himself.

"do it myself"
don't shame
your toddler
1-4 years

This is particularly important while he is trying out new skills. Without a doubt it will be painful for you to watch while your toddler pours his own juice and spills most of it on the floor or all over the table. However, freaking out and telling him that spilling is "bad" will pretty much ensure not only a timid toddler, but that you'll be pouring his juice until he's 10! Watch the words you use at this point, so that you don't make him ashamed of his actions. This is a difficult stage for both of you, and you want him to know you respect his independence.

"do it myself"
give him your attention

Carve out time to give your child your undivided attention. It does wonders for your child's self-worth because it sends the message that you think he's important and valuable.

It doesn't have to take a lot of time; it just means taking a moment to stop sorting through the mail if he's trying to talk with you, or turning off the TV long enough to answer a question. Make eye contact, so it's clear that you're really listening to what he's saying. When you're pressed for time, let your child know it without ignoring his needs. Say, "Tell me all about the picture you drew, and then when you're finished, I'll need to make our dinner."

"do it myself"

establish a few
reasonable rules   1-4 years

If you tell your child she has to eat her snack in the kitchen, don't let her wander around the family room with her crackers and fruit the next day. Knowing that certain family rules are set in stone will help her feel more secure. It may take constant repetition on your part, but she'll start to live by your expectations soon enough. Just be clear and consistent, and show her that you trust her and expect her to do the right thing.

"do it myself"

1-4 years a good rule of thumb

Let your toddler choose between just two possibilities,
since at this age too many options can be overwhelming.
For instance, ask her whether she wants to wear her polka-
dot dress or the striped one, or if she wants to paint or draw,
or whether she wants oatmeal or cold cereal for breakfast.
Once she has made her decision, follow through on it and
don't let her change her mind, because children need to
learn the consequences of decision making. She'll gain
confidence with each opportunity to make a decision.
Letting her know that you have faith in her judgment
increases your child's sense of self-worth.

new ventures

"do it myself"

1–4 years

Encourage your child to explore something new, such as trying a different food, finding a new pal, or going down the slide. Although there's always the possibility of failure, without some risk there's little opportunity for success.

"do it myself"
let him make mistakes . . .

The flip side of making choices and taking risks is that sometimes your child is bound to make mistakes. These are valuable lessons for your child's confidence. So go ahead and let him wear the snowsuit he insists on wearing even if it's balmy outside (just stash more appropriate clothing in your backpack). When he starts complaining that he's too hot, stifle your urge to say, "I told you so." Just whip out his favorite shorts and T-shirt and say something like, "How about wearing this since it's so warm?" That way his self-esteem won't sag and he'll understand that it's okay to make mistakes sometimes.

"do it myself"
. . . and act
for himself   1–4 years

Buy clothes that are easy to put on and pull off; get a stool
so he can wash his own hands and brush his teeth at the
sink; find a place for his toys and books that is within his
reach. By giving your toddler the
resources to take care of his
own needs, you'll help
foster independence
and pride in his ability
to do things for himself.

"do it myself"

give praise

One mom says: "It's sometimes too easy to tally up all the things a toddler does wrong, but everyone responds well to encouragement, so make an effort to acknowledge the good things your child does every day within her earshot." For instance, tell her dad, "Nina picked up all her toys today."

She'll bask in your praise and her dad's positive response. And be specific. Instead of saying, "Good job," say, "Thank you for waiting so patiently in line." This will enhance her self-worth and let her know exactly what she did right.

"do it myself"
listen to your child 1-4 years

I know, sometimes, he just goes on and on and . . . but get
in the habit of listening to what he is really saying. He needs
to know that his ideas and opinions matter—they don't
always count for a whole vote, but you do need to take
them on board. My father always used to say, "Sure we can
vote on it, but just remember, I pay the bills so my vote
counts 10 times!" Try to encourage your child to express
why he is sad, rather than just whining about it, and you will
both be happier. "I'm sad because we're leaving the park" in
a non-whiny voice will almost always get five extra minutes
of playtime; a tantrum when I tell him it's time to go, results
in an immediate escort to the car!

beyond
home

Your child is gaining independence at home—perhaps
sometimes even more than you'd like. But what about
beyond home? There is a whole world out there and,
more often than not, you'll want to show it to your child.
But leaving familiar surroundings, whether in your own
home town or even abroad, can be stressful for little
ones. How do you get your child to let go of your apron
strings (okay—I never wear an apron, but you know what
I mean) in these tricky situations? The following tips
should help you and your child encounter that world with
minimal discomfort. In addition, there are a few tips on
dealing with a lost child—a very real issue when that
apron-string holder turns into a fearless explorer.

keep a routine

Whether in a plane, train, or car, try to make sure your child's snack, meal, and nap times remain relatively consistent. Little ones are usually happiest in the early hours of the day, so if you're on vacation, try to get your sightseeing in then. Leave afternoons for naps, playtime, and cuddle time, and remind your child about the temporary status of this new accommodation. The happier your child is, the more likely he will be to let go of those apron strings and explore his new surroundings.

2–5 years **home away from home**

Going on vacation should be a fun experience for both
parent and child, but sometimes it can confuse or even
terrify a normally independent little one. Suddenly the
refrigerator is in a different place, or maybe there isn't one;
the bed is different, the curtains are different,
the TV is bigger or smaller; there are weird
noises above and below. The key is to
create a home away from home.

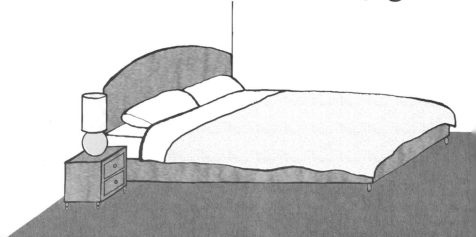

Bring familiar objects (okay, not the fridge)—blankets from home, maybe a pillow or two, and anything that your child might be used to smelling, like mom's lotion or a favorite soap (not the dog!). Having recognizable objects around will help your child to feel more secure in this new situation. Scheduling a visit to a local park, school, library, or even a fast-food restaurant may also be comforting to a novice traveler who is craving familiar surroundings.

the backpack

The baby backpack is a very common sight these days, but many parents are unaware that they hold children, some up to the age of four or even five (not my Buddha-belly boys, but some . . .). This is a great way to, first, keep your child safe in crowded situations like fairs or even supermarkets, but also to, believe it or not, foster independence. The child in the backpack will be able to explore unfamiliar places with you right there with him, and as he gets more accustomed to the situation at hand, will probably ask to get out and explore it for himself. That bird's eye view of the world goes a long way toward

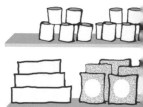

demystifying the situation. Imagine being only three feet high in a crowded world full of very tall people, your only view the backs of hairy legs? It would make me want to jump in my mother's arms, too!

2-5 years   **foreign food**

The web site *www.travelingwithchildren.com* offers some sound advice for coping with "foreign food." It recommends getting your child used to eating the sort of food that is readily available in foreign restaurants and at camping sites. In particular it is invaluable to get him used to eating cheese, since bread or biscuits with cheese, an apple, or tomato, makes a well-balanced meal and can be put together in seconds. Such a portable, widely available meal means that you don't need to spend ages worrying what to feed your little one when you're out and about.

let them run wild

2 years and up

One mom says, "I've noticed that it really helps when kids are allowed to feel like they have a say in the travel itinerary. A lot of times the 'traditional,' mostly inside, planned vacations aren't too great for the kids. Make sure you stop frequently on road trips to let the kids run around and play outside for a while. If you're staying at a hotel or in one location, find a local square, park, or pile of rocks that the kids can play in, run, scream, torture siblings, etc. It helps ease stress."

home
exchange

Another mom tried exchanging homes one summer and found it to be a great alternative to a hotel. "Consider a home exchange vacation, to both save money when visiting expensive cities and to have a comfortable base to return to after a day of sightseeing. Families with children have a much more relaxing vacation on an exchange than when cooped up in a hotel room. If you swap with another family with children of similar ages to your own, your children will have a whole new range of toys, books—and even local playmates!" This not only gives children the experience of another place, but it can encourage their independence by giving them a safe home away from home.

show them
the way

2 years and up

Prepare your children in advance for the trip you will be
taking. If you are traveling by car or plane, you can show
them on a map the route you will be taking. Even young
children enjoy looking at maps. Give them travel brochures
on the places you will be visiting, and check out some books
from your local library about where you will be going. There
are even special travel guides written specifically for children.

count down the days

2 years and up

Create anticipation for the family trip by starting a countdown calendar with a photo of the destination. Let kids make some choices while you are packing. Decide what type of clothing (preferably loose and comfortable), but allow them to choose their favorites and to pack a special toy. In a carry-on bag, pack some hard candies and gum, hand wipes, tissues, books, paper, markers in a small, sealed plastic bag, and perhaps a surprise toy for each child.

let the kids buy their own treats

4 years and up

At the beginning of the trip, give each child a dollar or two for each day. They are then responsible for buying all those little treats they want (like soda or a snack). They can keep any money they don't spend. "This keeps the kids from begging to buy everything they see," said one mom. "I find my children don't want as many snacks—they prefer to keep the cash! I spend less and don't have to deal with whining children!" Kids become much more adventurous and outgoing when they have their own money to spend and they learn about assessing the value of things. This can also work with smaller children, on a less "responsible" level—allowing them to pay for things, but not making them keep track of their cash.

how not to lose your child!

2 years and up

In our efforts to let our children explore the world, a very real danger exists—that of losing them. My own son, a very independent seven-year-old, was doing great at the airport until we got to the baggage claim. Suddenly, he was gone. I was frantic, until he was found talking to a nice woman. Even the most conscientious of parents can lose track of a child—particularly one who likes to explore. One parent found a good solution: "In case of separation, every second counts! When traveling through airports or other crowded places, I lace two 'jingle bells' to the toes of my son's shoes. I also hang a small plastic whistle on a string around his neck, to be used *only* if he gets separated from us. Finally, I carry a recent, full-length photo of him in his standard travel outfit —a quick way for people to recognize him in a busy place!"

other tracking devices

2 years and up

Other good ideas to keep track of a child (useful whether you're on vacation or just going to the store) include: dressing all your children in similar colors for each outing, so that they are easier to spot in a crowd; getting the local hospital to make up an ID bracelet for your child; making up a note with your child's information on it, so that she can bring it to a customer service desk or to a security officer.

mom's
day off

It is every mother's dream to have a day to herself.
Whether you use the day to get errands done or just to
hang out with a friend at her child-free house, all moms
deserve some time off every so often. Heck, sometimes
I didn't even want a whole day to myself, but just 10
minutes to shower without two children sitting on the
floor of the bathroom keeping an eye on me . . . literally!
But what happens when your vision of the perfect day is
ruined by guilt and the memory of the screaming baby
you left behind? Nothing plays with our psyches more
than the sound of, "Mommy, come back" from a wailing
child still ringing in our ears hours later. These tips can
help you deal with the inevitable tantrum when you
try to let go and, in many cases, can prevent it from
happening in the first place.

"where's the baby?" 6 months–1 year

Drop a lightweight cloth over your baby's head, ask, "Where's the baby?" and pull the cloth away again, grinning and saying, "There you are!" Soon your baby will delight at pulling the cloth off and laughing. The cloth can also be placed over your own head and you can ask, "Where's Mommy?" Or play peek-a-boo. As you hide your face with your hands, or hide your body on the other side of the couch or around the corner of the room, your baby learns that you still exist, even though you're out of sight.

mom's day off

6 months–2 years

give your baby plenty of space

If you hover over her all the time, she'll get the idea that you're afraid of leaving her by herself and that there's actually something to fear from being alone. Don't worry about leaving her in her crib or her infant seat while you are taking a shower or doing the laundry. You could play music or a book-on-tape while you're out of the room, to give her something to fill the empty space. Just make sure that wherever you leave her is safe and child-proofed and that you can hear her from wherever you are.

leave while
baby is awake

6 months–2 years

Waking up in the middle of the night to a strange (or even a familiar but unexpected) sitter can be terrifying. It is, I know, so much easier to leave while he is asleep, but this will get you nowhere in the future. As your child takes fewer and fewer naps during the day, it is more likely that you will have to leave him at some point when he's awake. Start doing it right from the beginning. Hand him over to the sitter and, if he's a toddler or preschooler, tell him when you're coming back. If he's still an infant, coo over him a bit and leave with a smile on your face.

mom's day off

practice being
out of view

1-3 years

If your toddler is playing in another room out of your sight and starts to make a fuss, instead of immediately dropping what you are doing and rushing to him, try calling to him instead, "I'm right here!" or singing a favorite song. This will prove to your child that, even when you aren't right in his sight, you are still around. If your child becomes inconsolable, go to him of course; but if he is merely fussing a bit, then sing a little, go to him and prove you're there, and then go back to folding laundry or whatever you were doing. Doing this several times through the day is essential to make him a believer, and will give you time to practice being out of your child's sight before you take that two-hour trip to the market on your own.

if separation
isn't working

1–3 years

Sometimes even a baby who was "easy to leave" suddenly becomes a toddler who is separation-sensitive. If your little one isn't taking well to your absences, you might try more creative ways of staying happy yourself, which— temporarily at least— don't involve leaving your baby.

95

develop a strong attachment

1-3 years

Singing, playing, reading, and talking together all help build a strong, loving bond between you and your child and help him feel more secure. And the more secure he is, the less he'll worry about being abandoned.

don't give in
to crying

It's so hard not to give in to the wailing and crying that are bound to ensue when you attempt to leave, but you must be strong. Ease the transition by having the baby-sitter come 20 or 30 minutes ahead of time. That way, the baby-sitter and the child can get involved in something while you're still there (gathering your things, or whatever). Your child will hear your voice, but still will be interacting happily with the sitter. Then you can make your quick good-byes and head out. If he still wails when you leave, keep going. If he knows he can get you to stay by crying, you'll never get out of the house!

use some distractions

My biggest failing as a parent (okay, one of them) is that when I hear my little one wailing for me, I go back to him again and again, making the situation worse. I keep saying things like, "I'm coming back, I promise" and "I won't be gone forever." It's horrible for both of us. So to minimize such difficulties during separations I have learned not to make such a big deal out of leaving in the first place. Try to downplay leaving and have someone distract your child (with a game or favorite toy) after you say good-bye. He may cry as you leave, but quickly will stop and show interest in whoever is watching him once you are completely out of sight.

establish a
good-bye routine

2-5 years

One youngster has a short routine that she follows whenever she leaves her mother. She gives her mother a

big bear hug and a kiss. Her mother then says, "I love you, and I'll see you later." The child then waves good-bye, secure in the knowledge that she will be reunited with her mom soon.

mom's day off

2-5 years   **don't berate yourself**

For some kids, distress is simply one sign of their attachment to you. On the other hand, don't be concerned if your child doesn't show distress as you leave the house; it's not a sign of a lack of attachment to you, just the reflection of a different sort of personality.

expect lapses

My five-year-old was so ready for kindergarten. He knew his way around the school, thanks to the many events we had attended for his older brothers and sister. Then, the summer before he was due to start school, we moved and all of a sudden he had a new school to learn, new teachers, and all sorts of new faces. He ran to his classroom on the first day of school and, on entering the busy room, had a complete meltdown, crying harder and longer than he had for a very long time. It was an unexpected reaction because he was so confident and excited for so long. Children from three to six years of age may become upset seemingly out of the blue. Possible causes include disruptions in the family routine or other difficulties at home or perhaps at school. With your child and her teacher or other caregiver, work to uncover and address the cause of your child's anxiety.

School!

Heading off to school can be a wonderful experience or a terrifying one, for both parent and child. There is nothing worse than getting your child all prepared for school— new clothes, new lunch box, a song or two during the car ride there—only to have him scream and cry your name as you leave. My youngest son was so distraught over his first preschool experience that for the first two weeks he sat at the window looking for our car to come and rescue him. It's a horrible feeling to leave your child while he is begging you to come back, but sometimes you have to do it. These tips should help both of you cope a little better.

prepare him

School!

3-5 years

Explain to your child ahead of time what is going to happen so that he knows what to expect. Be specific about what he will be doing at day care or preschool. Include things like eating, drinking, resting, and bathrooming in your explanation so that your child will understand that these basic needs will be met.

School!

3–5 years   **be firm**

Explain where you will be and what you will be doing while you are away from your little one. State it matter-of-factly, as something grown-ups have to do. Going to work is not a choice for you, and likewise going to school or day care is not a choice for your child.

trial visits

School!

3-5 years

Take your child on several trial visits to the school or day care center before he starts going there regularly. This will give him the chance to gradually get to know his teachers, the other children who attend, and the routine.

school!

3-5 years

practice saying
the names

Help your child learn to say the names of his teachers and
the names of the other children in the preschool. By staying
with him for a while on those first couple of days, you can
help him get to know the people he will be hanging out with
while you're gone. Then, after school, make a point of asking
your child about the kids or teachers at school. Find out,
through your child, what he's interested in. Also, ask him
to discover certain things about the other children while
he's there, like, "What's Jimmy's favorite color?" This will
give him a mom- or dad-related task during the day, but will
keep him involved in school. Inviting a few of the children
over on the weekends also can help him to settle in well
and be eager to go back to school on Monday morning.

ensure your child gets enough sleep

School!

3-5 years

Most preschool children need about 11 hours of sleep a night. Kindergartners and first-graders need 8 to 12 hours, and young grade-schoolers need 8 to 10 hours. Getting enough sleep will alleviate any initial crankiness and make your child less prone to outbursts relating to your departure—or anything else, for that matter.

School!

avoid the morning rush

Choose outfits and pack lunch bags the night before.
Make a simple picture schedule to help your child learn
what must be done in the morning before you leave.
For example, a drawing of some clothes, a bowl of cereal,
and a toothbrush will remind your child about getting
dressed, eating breakfast, and brushing his teeth. Let him
check off each chore as he completes it. One other helpful
hint: each night I summon each child with his or her
backpack. I then look through the backpack for any papers
I have to sign (there are always a few) and set it up for the
next morning. This avoids the morning, "Mom, can you sign . . . "
or "Mom, I need money for . . . "

give her something of yours

School!

3-5 years

Your child might feel more secure if she has something of yours to hold on to during the day, like a scarf or glove. A photograph of you tucked in her cubby or lunchbox is comforting, too, and reminds her that you're really not that far away.

School!

try to arrive early . . .

When you take your child in to preschool, arrive early
enough so that you won't have to dash off immediately.
Allow sufficient time to share any important information
about your little one with the teachers. You might want to
read a short book with your child, or play with him for a
couple of minutes before saying good-bye. Set a limit on
how long you will stay. For example, you might tell your
child that you will read one book or play with blocks for
five minutes before you have to leave.

...but don't linger too long

3–5 years

Lingering at preschool only adds more anxiety to the situation. Encourage your child to go to the window and wave to you as you leave. Never sneak out without saying good-bye to your child.

promise to return

Let your child know when you will be coming back, using the preschool's schedule to mark off chunks of the day. For example, you might say, "I will be back after you wake up from your nap and have your snack."

be consistent

A child who is just beginning school or day care is very susceptible to change. Keeping their schedule as consistent as possible is essential, especially early on. If an emergency comes up and your pick-up plans change during the day, call your childcare provider as soon as possible and ask him or her to explain the change to your child. Make sure you don't pick up your child at different times every day, though. Try and keep it consistent so that he isn't looking for you at 1 P.M. when you won't actually be coming to collect him until 4 P.M. I made the mistake of picking up my child early on his first few days of day care, thinking I was doing him a favor, but I only made him desperate to see me right after lunch on days when I couldn't get out of work early.

apron-string
Syndrome

Sometimes it doesn't matter what the situation is—your child will be unhappy whether you are leaving for a few days, the work day, or even just driving the car while he is in the backseat. Sometimes as moms and dads, you feel like you can't go anywhere for fear of incurring the wrath of your precious little one. But there are ways to get through it. First, you must remember to be patient. Second, remember that some day they will be embarrassed to be seen with you, so enjoy their clinginess while you can. And third, accept that sometimes you just have to leave—but sometimes you can make alternate plans. Couple this with the following tips and those clingy early years should be a little easier.

sing along

Help him understand his feelings by singing, one mom suggests (to the tune of "The Farmer in the Dell"): "I want my mama to come back, I want my mama to come back, I want my mama to come back soon, I want my mama to come back!" His caregiver can also sing soothingly, "You want your mama to come back." The Hap Palmer recording of "My Mama Comes Back" would also be a good song to play and sing for him.

apron-string syndrome
enlist the caregiver's help

2-5 years

It's a difficult transition for most children, to go from being with mom all day to being with someone else. Most caregivers are very prepared for a child's anxiety, though, and will know what to do in such a situation. If you know of specific things that will help your child feel better, tell the caregiver. Ask her to hold your little one in her arms more over these next few weeks, and to use gentle back rubs at nap time. Your little guy needs extra physical displays of affection to get through this time while he comes to terms with the reality that you always come back to get him.

apron-string syndrome
reassure her
with activity
2–5 years

At home, carry out lots of leisurely, physical, routine activities to reassure her how precious she is to you. Rub her down after a bath with a soft bath towel. Then wrap her in your arms and nibble kisses on her head and face.

apron-string syndrome
ensure childcare
stability

2-5 years

Find out whether there have been any changes in the staff at the child care center. Babies in particular need very stable care situations. They like the same folks to care for them and could be thrown for a loop if that changes. If you can, try to get your younger child involved in a "home care" situation where maybe one or two moms care for children together. This will keep the care consistent. At the same time, if you must go to a larger center, find out what their policy is about changing staff. If there are at least two teachers (or helpers) in a room, your child will know at least one person if someone leaves.

apron-string syndrome
don't expect
the impossible
2-5 years

Do not initiate any new routines—such as potty training or
always eating with a spoon—at this time. As your child
begins to hear your reassuring
words and sees that you keep
your promises day after
day by coming to pick him
up, he will get less upset.
Meanwhile: lots of cuddling,
lots of familiar, pleasurable
routines, and lots of
patience.

apron-string syndrome

make connections . . .

One mom says she couldn't even be separated from her
child in the car without him having a massive tantrum.
She suggests giving your child a substitute: if he can't have
you while you're traveling, a stand-in will do, at least until
you get to your destination. A hanky with your perfume
sprayed on it, a picture of the two of you doing something
together, or even your handbag (with all dangerous and
potentially messy items removed) will do—anything that
makes a connection between you and your little one
without distracting you as you drive.

apron-string syndrome
. . . and funny faces

2–5 years

The same mom also suggests making the most of red lights.
When you're at a stop sign or red light, angle your rearview
mirror so your toddler can see you, and make funny faces at
her. You may brighten her mood enough to last the length
of the ride. If you're able, reach back and squeeze her arm
or leg to let her know you're thinking of her.

apron-string syndrome

acknowledge the fear

Some of your toddler's worries are entirely normal and denying them would be unrealistic. If he's afraid of losing you in a store, for example, tell him that this idea scares you just as much as it scares him; tell him that's precisely why you watch him so closely, and that's why he should always be able to see you when you're together in any public place. But do remind him that when you drop him off at the baby-sitter's, the situation is very different because he is in a friendly and safe place—and that you always return and pick him up again.

talk it out

Toddlers have active imaginations, but limited vocabularies, so they may have trouble describing what frightens them. With some coaching from you, she may better articulate her feelings. Is she sad, angry, scared? Many parents find that just helping their children find words to describe their fears can ease anxiety.

apron-string syndrome
give him a break

Some parents believe they need to discourage "clinginess," not realizing that it's more important to allow the child to cling while working to build up his confidence and self-esteem. Forcing your child to pet a dog, or to sleep in the dark without a night light, won't ease his fear. At this age, he's probably better off conquering his fears at his own pace.

plan ahead

2–5 years

If your child tends to get nervous in large gatherings or new situations, she'll probably do better if you tell her exactly what to expect. Mention that you're going to a new place, and that she will get to meet some new people there. Be positive about the experience. Ask her if she'd like to bring along a favorite blanket or her stuffed bear for company. And when you get there, hang out with her until she feels comfortable, even if that means she spends an hour on your lap while she adjusts to the situation.

further reading

BRAZELTON, T. BERRY.
Touchpoints: Your Child's Emotional and Behavioral Development: Birth–3: The Essential Reference for the Early Years.
Boulder, CO.: Perseus Publishing, 1992.

IOVINE, VICKI.
The Girlfriends' Guide to Toddlers: A Survival Manual to the "Terrible Twos" (And Ones and Threes) from the First Step, the First Potty and the First Word ("No") to the Last Blankie.
New York: Perigee, 1999.

SEEFELDT, CAROL.
Early Childhood Curriculum: Current Findings in Theory and Practice.
New York: Teachers College Press, 1999.

SEEFELDT, CAROL, AND GALPER, ALICE.
Active Experiences for Active Children.
Englewood Cliffs, N.J.: Prentice Hall, 1999.

USEFUL WEB SITES
www.thumbguard.com
www.travelingwithchildren.com
www.hoppalmer.com

notes

Acknowledgments

I would like to thank my children, my husband John Hogan, my mother, and Rebecca Saraceno and Mandy Greenfield for all their help and encouragement.

127

index